BEGINNERS

A Very Simple Step-By-Step Guide
To Crocheting For Beginners

JUSTIN SUSAN

Table of Contents

CHAPTER ONE 3
   INTRODUCTION 3
CHAPTER TWO 4
   PURPOSE OF CROCHET 4
CHAPTER THREE 8
   CROCHET PATTERNS 8
CHAPTER FOUR 12
   WHO CAN CROCHET 12
CHAPTER FIVE 15
   HOW TO MAKE SCARF WITH CROCHET 15
CHAPTER SIX 21
   CROCHET HEADSCARF COMMANDS 21
THE END 27

CHAPTER ONE

INTRODUCTION

Crochet is a needlework method achieved the use of a crochet hook plus fiber or different similar cloth. Maximum typically, this cloth is yarn or crochet thread, but it might also be fabric, cord, wire, or other progressive cloth.

No one is precisely positive when and where in the craft of crochet originated, however the phrase comes from croc, the middle French phrase for curved instrument or hook.

CHAPTER TWO

PURPOSE OF CROCHET

The maximum popular goal in crochet is apparent: Crochet lovers desire to complete crochet tasks, which might be normally objects which might be useful, attractive or beneficial in a few manner. Famous tasks include afghans, toddler blankets, child booties, scarves, hats, granny squares, shawls, purses, tote bags and others. It is possible to crochet an expansion of different matters, including jewelry, socks, and curtains.

Also, it is possible to crochet various components to use in other items. For example, crochet trims and edgings are famous projects; you could observe them to crocheted objects, knitted items, and sewn objects (together with readymade save-offered gadgets.) for example, you could buy a few socks, towels and / or pillowcases, and add a crocheted edging to each.

No longer all crocheters are worried with completing crochet initiatives. There are different dreams, blessings and advantages to crochet except simply the tasks.

The basic Unit in Crochet: A Crochet stitch

Each crochet project is constituted of crochet stitches. The fundamental crochet stitches are as follows:

- The chain sew

- The slip stitch

- The unmarried crochet sew

- The double crochet sew

- The half of double crochet sew

- The treble crochet sew

- The double treble crochet stitch

- The triple treble crochet sew

Crochet sew styles

Crochet fanatics can combine the fundamental stitches in diverse methods to create interesting sew patterns. It is possible to create many special consequences; sew styles may be lacy or stable, colorful or monochromatic, patterned or simple. Several famous crochet sew patterns are as follows:

- Shell stitch
- V sew
- Cluster stitch

CHAPTER THREE

CROCHET PATTERNS

A crochet pattern is a hard and fast of commands for crocheting an item, or once in a while a related set of gadgets.

In which to find Crochet styles

You could discover crochet patterns in lots of places. Masses of patterns are available totally free on the net. There are numerous crochet books that incorporate groupings of crochet styles.

There are magazines committed to crochet, and also craft magazines and fashionable interest magazines in which you'll additionally locate crochet patterns blanketed.

How to examine a Crochet pattern

Typically, crochet designers write their styles the usage of abbreviations to store space. For you to examine a crochet sample, you need to understand this and make yourself familiar with the abbreviations blanketed within the pattern.

You will commonly be capable of locate the abbreviations in a logical location. With the styles we've got published on our website, we put the abbreviations near the top of each sample, before the commands. If you're sample is from a book or magazine, you'll commonly find the abbreviations listed somewhere within the front or the back of the e-book.

Similarities and differences among Crochet and Knitting

People often confuse crochet with knitting. The techniques do proportion commonplace factors;

for instance, each crocheters and knitters make use of yarn to create their tasks. It is possible to create comparable styles of projects with either technique: Afghans, shawls, hats, scarves, and so on.

At a glance, you could inform whether or not someone is knitting or crocheting through searching on the equipment (s)he's the use of. If (s)he is the use of a hook, (s)he's crocheting; if she's using pointed needles, or perhaps a round knitting needle, (s)he is knitting.

CHAPTER FOUR

WHO CAN CROCHET

If you've by no means crocheted earlier than, you might be questioning if it is a profitable hobby, or if it's something you have got the proper skill set to get concerned with.

No special talent is needed to crochet and, you possibly have the proper skill set as well.

The coolest news: pretty much all and sundry can crochet. There are younger youngsters who crochet and extremely old human beings too. Each men and women crochet. People from all over the global crochet. People with disabilities crochet and that even consist of blind people. Poor people crochet, and so do wealthy people.

With crochet, there are only a few limitations to entry, however there are some considerations you may need to be privy to before you get commenced.

Crochet may be either a solitary hobby, or a set hobby. It works well both manners.

If you'd want to get social together with your crocheting, there are bunches of methods to connect with different crochet lovers.

CHAPTER FIVE

HOW TO MAKE SCARF WITH CROCHET

Crochet patterns don't get any less difficult than this one! This is just about the most primary crochet scarf pattern you can ask for, which makes it the proper crochet accent sample for novices. Now not most effective is that this pattern and clean way to make a headband, but it is also written for those who do not have huge enjoy analyzing crochet styles. There are not abbreviations and there are a lot of suggestions to help you along the manner.

Crochet Stitches

There are handiest two crochet stitches you may need to understand for this crochet headscarf pattern: the chains sew and the unmarried crochet stitch. If you haven't discovered how to do those stitches yet, ensure that you exercise those first after which come again to this sample.

What you will want

Gear

- Crochet hook, size ok

- Tapestry needle

Supplies

- 5 oz. /150 grams of worsted weight yarn

Finished headband size

This headscarf measures 84 inches (seven feet) long by using four inches huge. Scarves can range in length without altering function so do not worry if yours is not pretty the equal. You'll learn as you go.

Gauge

8 single crochet stitches = 3 inches.

At the same time as it's tempting to leap proper in and start making the headband, it is top to get into the habit of checking your gauge. To do that, crochet a gauge swatch measuring as a minimum 4 inches square (larger is higher). Make the swatch in single crochet sew the use of the exact same yarn and crochet hook you may use to crochet your headscarf. Degree the middle 3 inches of the swatch to look how many stitches according to inch you are operating with that particular combination of hook and yarn.

When you have extra than 8 stitches per 3 inches, it manner that your stitches are smaller than deliberate and your headband will be smaller than the instance. Try making a brand new swatch with a larger crochet hook.

Likewise, if you find which you have fewer than eight stitches in line with three inches, it way your stitches are larger than planned. If so, your headband is probably to turn out much longer than supposed; you furthermore might chance strolling out of yarn because larger stitches will use up extra yarn and create a bigger headscarf. Try making a brand new swatch with a smaller crochet hook.

CHAPTER SIX

CROCHET HEADSCARF COMMANDS

Pull out duration of yarn measuring at least 6 inches or longer; go away this duration unworked and make a slip knot after that point. Then, operating with the end attached to the ball of yarn, crochet a protracted starting chain of 224 chain stitches.

Use stitch markers every 10 or 20 stitches as you figure, to preserve higher song and make it less complicated to depend on the cease.

Row One: paintings a single crochet stitch within the second chain out of your hook.

After crocheting your chain, you'll have an active loop nonetheless for your hook. Do not rely your energetic loop. Start counting with the primary chain after the lively loop.

Keep working single crochet stitches the entire manner throughout your starting chain. Work one unmarried crochet sew into every chain sew until you attain the end. While you get to the stop, count the single crochet stitches to ensure you have got a complete of 223. Once more, sew markers are beneficial here.

In case your count is off, you may have introduced or subtracted a sew, which regularly takes place at the beginning and stop of rows. Get the count number proper from Row One on or your headband won't have even edges.

Subsequent, crochet one chain sew on the stop of the row to use as a turning chain. Then, flip your work horizontally so you can work returned throughout the piece.

Row two: when you look at the top of the row of single crochet stitches you made, you will see that each sews has a loop on the top. Whilst you work your single crochet stitches from this factor on, be careful to paintings through each of these loops collectively.

Working through each loops, paintings a single crochet sew into the ultimate unmarried crochet sew you made in row one. Preserve running one unmarried crochet sew into each unmarried crochet sew, all the way throughout the row.

Be sure to count number your stitches and make sure you've got 223 stitches in the row. (Bear in mind to apply sew markers to help hold your rely correct—retaining be counted is so critical for a success venture!) Work one chain sew at the quit of the row and flip the paintings over so that you can work again throughout once more.

Rows three and Up: Repeat Row two till your headscarf is the preferred width. While you crochet the last row, do now not paintings a turning chain afterward due to the fact now it's time to complete your work in preference to turning it over and continuing.

How to end off

Go away a duration of yarn on the cease measuring at the least six inches. Cut the yarn, taking care now not to drop your energetic loop. Wrap the reduce duration of yarn around your hook, clutch it with the hook, and pull it the entire manner through the energetic loop. Supply it a mild tug to ensure that it's far tight and could no longer come undone. Thread the cut cease of this yarn onto a tapestry needle and use it to weave on your ends.

THE END